# IDIOMS

by
Bhuvan Bhadra

Waldenhouse Publishers, Inc.
Walden, Tennessee

# IDIOMS

Published by Waldenhouse Publishers, Inc.
100 Clegg Street, Signal Mountain, Tennessee 37377 USA
423-886-2721 www.waldenhouse.com
Printed in the United States of America
ISBN: 978-1-947589-10-0 case bound        $24.95
ISBN: 978-1-947589-13-1 perfect bound    $16.95
Library of Congress Control Number: 2019901482
Thirty-one frequently used English language idioms illustrated with thirty-one humorous line drawings created by a ten-year-old boy reared in a home of blended cultures. He uses cartoon style drawings to depict the literal meanings of English idioms and to elucidate the concepts of formulaic language and figurative meanings. -- Provided by publisher
HUM001000 HUMOR / Form / Comic Strips & Cartoons
LAN016000 LANGUAGE ARTS & DISCIPLINES / Linguistics / Semantics
EDU029080 EDUCATION / Teaching Methods & Materials / Language Arts
Century Gothic on LSI Premium 70#
Type and Design by Karen Paul Stone

To

# Mami and Daddy,
I love you so much!

Bhuvan

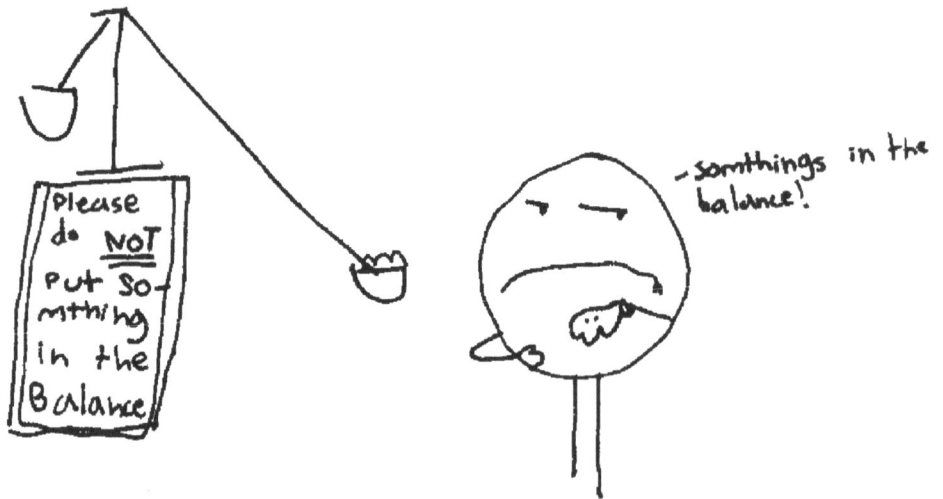

Something is in the balance

Break the Ice

# Rat Race

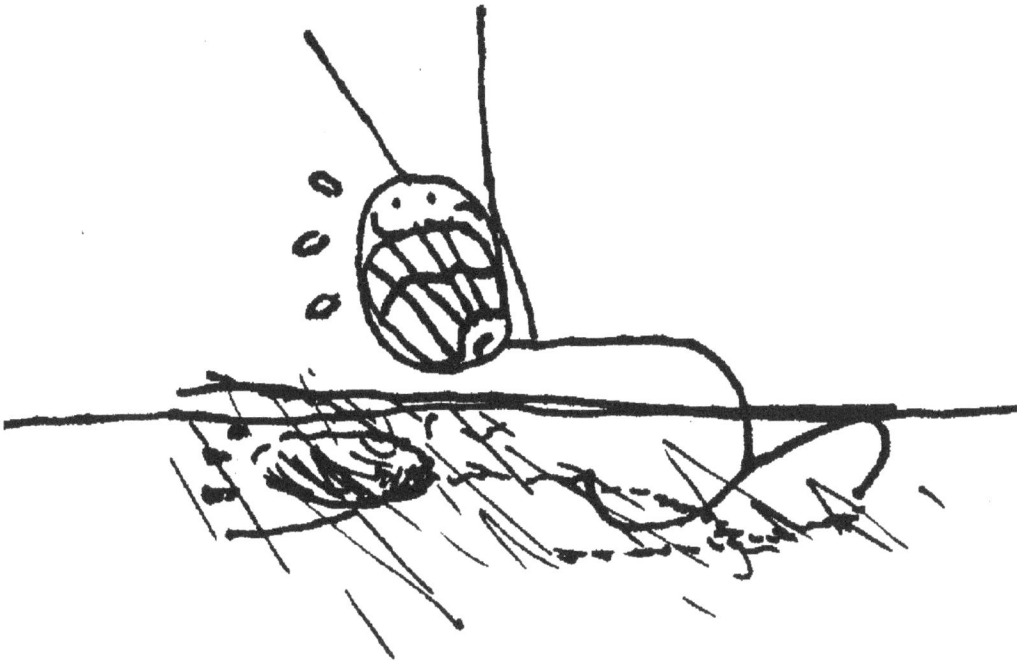

Afraid of your own shadow

Add fuel to the fire

Air your dirty laundry

It's on the house

A little birdie told me

On pins and needles

It's out of the box

You took a haircut on that one

Chip on your shoulder

Shoot yourself in the foot

Put lipstick on a pig

To have egg on your face

The apple doesn't fall far from the tree

Put your foot in your mouth

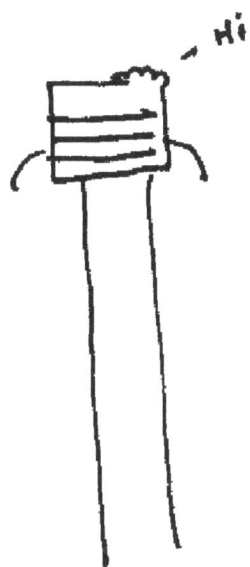

Cakewalk

Get your feet wet

Skeletons in the closet

Out of the woods

Walking on eggshells

A wolf in sheep's clothing

Last straw

Bury your head in the sand

Bad apple

Blind as a bat

Break a leg

Bury the hatchet

Bring home the bacon

Fall between the cracks

www.ingramcontent.com/pod-product-compliance
Lightning Source LLC
Chambersburg PA
CBHW060901090426
42738CB00023B/3484